Willpower

How to Discover Your Internal Strength and the Self Discipline Mindset Needed to Accomplish Your Goals

Russell Davis

Table of Contents

Introduction

Imagine yourself as a four-year-old in a world filled with awe and beauty. There's a table with a delicious looking marshmallow on it. A researcher-scientist informs you that he will be back in a while, and you can feast on the marshmallow whenever you like. You almost rub your hands in a glee. Hold on, the geeky looking researcher has a catch. If you manage to hold on until he comes back, you get two marshmallows.

Now, you're caught in a huge dilemma – one marshmallow immediately, or two later? A battle of sorts ensues in your mind. You are in a quandary now – to do or not to do? There is every attempt to ignore the marshmallow, but there's no denying the prospect is tempting. A single move now and you can taste the mushy, sugary marshmallow right away. Will be you able to last until the researcher returns?

This is the exact famous experiment conducted by psychologist Walter Mischel to study how successfully young children resist temptation, and the impact it has in later years on their academics, career and personal life. It may seem far-fetched to you to be able to deduce how well-adjusted and successful a person can turn out to be based on his/her ability to delay gratification as a kid. However, the results of this

Getting back to the experiment, a few children could resist after all in their quest to enjoy two marshmallows later, while others opted for instant gratification. The ones who delayed fulfillment for a good fifteen minutes distracted themselves by singing or looking the other way.

 It was nearly two decades after the experiment was conducted that it became such a psychological rage. Walter Mischel chanced upon the idea of following up with his subjects to determine how they were faring as late adolescents. The startling results revealed that those four-year-olds who were able to delay gratification outperformed their peers in almost every sphere. They were predicted to witness success in almost all life areas.

These kids grew up to demonstrate higher self-esteem, lower instances of drug abuse, better academic performance, and higher fitness levels. Not just that, these kids were also scored high on popularity compared to children who weren't able to resist instant gratification.

Research in the psychological domain has consistently pointed to the fact that among all known human abilities, willpower is the most critical for achieving a variety of life's outcomes. Self-control is the pathway to predicting an individual's success. The more successfully a person can delay immediate or small gratifications for higher goals, the better are his/her chances of achieving success in life.

Willpower, self-control, the ability to resist temptation - whatever you may call it – is important for better health, higher work productivity, more fulfilling relationships, and lower stress levels. A person's social success is also keenly impacted by his/her willpower. For instance, when our will tires out, we tend to say and do things which we later regret.

Some experts also believe that willpower is a much more reliable indicator of our success in life than the hyped Intelligence Quotient. It can help predict our college grade average and other academic success measurements more effectively than IQ.

Talent, intelligence, and skills may hold you good for a while; however one does have to put in serious hard work to get there, which is why the ones who make serious effort often outperform the skilled yet lazy folks. You will wonder how that boy you thought was below average and couldn't do math correctly in class has outperformed the seemingly gifted class mathematician. It is nothing but sheer effort and practice.

Pick up the biography of any popular athlete, scientist, performer or world leader. They possess the initial talent yes, loads of it. But so do the others. What separates them from everyday people is not their talent, but a sheer willpower to chase their dreams through a series of hardships. Giving up isn't an option for them. Professor Angela Duckworth (University of Pennsylvania) has rightly stated that "programs that build self-discipline may be the royal road to building academic achievement."

Willpower or grit is one of the most vital resources to help you fulfill all that you are aiming for in life. Contrary to popular perception, willpower is not just required in the most challenging life situations. You really don't have to wait to climb a mountain for exercising your willpower.

It can be put to use in daily situations such as focusing on your work when the urge to check your Facebook feed or messenger is high. It can be exercised by saying no to an extra piece of cookie you know is not good for you. These are seemingly small wins that go a huge way in helping you emerge victorious in the game of life.

Adhering to deadlines, studying diligently for an examination or going to the gymnasium every day isn't the easiest thing to do. There are several more comfortable and less demanding trajectories. However, are they worth it in the long run? You may find the prospect of watching a movie or going out with your friends instead of studying before an examination highly enticing. Will it help you bag good grades? Will you able to opt for majors of your choice?

Willpower is the simple distinction between a student who graduates with flying colors and one who struggles to complete school. It is the point of difference between two similarly talented workers, only one of whom gets promoted. What seems enticing or irresistible may not always be right or good for you. Developing willpower is segregating short term comforts from long-term benefits.

When you understand the science and art of willpower, it is easier to use it to create a life of your dreams. The concept of willpower had grown leaps and bounds in the last few decades. There are several handy willpower tools that you can now use to build your willpower muscle, delay gratification, achieve academic success, fulfill your life goals and overcome everyday challenges.

The book aims to gather knowledge about various proven willpower development techniques and deliver it to you in a practical, easy to understand and actionable manner. Use it like you would use an instructions manual for simply reading it is not doing justice to yourself.

Integrate these simple yet proven techniques into your daily life, and witness the changes. You will get everything you want if you are prepared to make the right (and not just comfortable) choices. In fact, you will find it much easier to achieve your goals if you simply flex your willpower muscles. And once you start practicing it consciously, it will become a natural part of you. Doing the right thing or doing what's good for you in the long run will become second nature, an easy choice.

Here's to your journey of turning into a willpower maestro!

Chapter 1: Recognizing Your Weaknesses

Congratulations on surviving beyond the introduction to open your willpower account. No one on this planet is born without weaknesses. The world is filled with people who are imperfect and come with a bunch of shortcomings. However, none of us is born with a weakness we cannot challenge or change. There are startling examples of people from all fields who have successfully managed to turn their limitations on their head to achieve success. These folks have mastered the art of turning their limitations into strengths by sheer determination or willpower.

Do you know the concept of 10,000 hours? For those not in the know, it states that when a person spends 10,000 hours practicing something he/she isn't good at, he/she actually converts the weakness into a skill. Turning your negatives into positives requires you to identify or recognize your weakness.

You will hear a lot of people spouting the 'fact' that we must focus on our strengths and not our weaknesses. This may not be the best approach when it comes to fulfilling your life goals through will-power. The approach is general and simplistic, to put it mildly. The right approach is to figure out your strengths and weaknesses with respect to your goals.

Take for instance; you want to be an author in the digital media age. Now, a simplistic strengths and weaknesses approach will ask you focus on your strength - writing. However, an approach that matches your goals will urge you to do the exact opposite, and grow in areas which you need to develop, other than writing, to become a published author.

Let us say, if you want to publish independently, you ought to know cover design creation, marketing techniques and social media tools for promoting the book. You don't just need to focus on your strength but also have to work on your weaknesses for fulfilling your goals.

This is exactly how you should view the strengths and weaknesses model. Identify or recognize your pluses and minuses with respect to your life goals, which make it easier for you to work on your weaknesses.

So, how exactly does one recognize their weaknesses to overcome them? Here are some practical and highly effective techniques.

Redefine Your Weaknesses

Weakness might not always be the best label for your areas of improvement. What one perceives as his/her weakness may not be as defeating as they believe it to be. When you feel you can get better at some areas or aspects in your life, you are simply stating to yourself that you aren't as strong in these areas as you are in others.

We tend to believe and talk about everything related to us in absolutes. "I am so bad at speaking to an audience" or "I can barely draft a mail" or "I suck at creativity." What we do is exaggerate the situation by referring to it in absolutes rather than being realistically moderate. Weakness can have a slightly negative connotation to it. Rather than viewing something as your weakness, identify it as an area of improvement, which will help you work on it more effectively.

This will keep you focused on the steps you need to take for overcoming your weakness and realizing your goals. We need to realize that weaknesses are not permanent truths but temporary situations that can be changed to achieve our goals.

There can be several areas of improvement or development such as enhancing your social skills or mastering professional attributes/skills or showing more restraint with high-calorie food. The ability need not be anything large, it can be as simple as the solving math problems faster or being a better baseball catcher.

Often, our weaknesses are nothing but false, self-imposed limitations. In our limited, cagey thinking, we term things we aren't very good at as weaknesses. This self-labels stick with us for life, and we give up control over it. For instance, when you say to yourself that you are pathetic at making presentations in front of an audience, you accept the self-imposed limitation as your fate, without making any real effort to overcome your stage fright.

However, when you perceive these so-called limitations as an area of growth, you pull yourself up to work towards them by showing sheer willpower or determination. You act in control of your strengths and limitations, rather than accepting it as your unchanging reality.

Ask Your Family and Friends For Honest Feedback

The most honest and genuine feedback about our strengths and weaknesses can be obtained from people who know us well. Go ahead and actively solicit feedback from your family and friends about your true strengths and limitations.

Ask them to be honest, which in turn will help you work on your growth areas. If possible, ask for specific instances where they think you could've handled the situation in a better or different manner. The limitations can be everything from habits to skills to personality traits.

Pro tip – one of the best ways to do this (though it may sound ridiculous) is by undertaking this exercise via email just like you would do it at your workplace. Non-face to face communication doesn't make the feedback giver feel pressurized. It also gives them time to think their responses through and lets them give a more honest feedback. The bonus, you'll have everything documented in writing for future reference and analysis.

What do people normally request you to do for them? Do you constantly find people approaching you with requests for drafting their cover letter or resume? There, you may be a sharp and articulate writer. Note, what people generally ask you to do can be a reliable indication of your strengths. Do you find your playing agony aunt to your friends? You may be a great listener, known for their sound judgment and wise suggestions.

In the same vein, people may avoid coming to you for certain things, which can be perceived as your areas of improvement. What is it that people will generally avoid coming to you for? Think about the last time your manager shied away from entrusting a particular task to you or something that your co-workers hesitate to approach you for. When working in a team, what tasks are not assigned to you? This will give you a good idea about your areas of growth.

Make a List of Your Strengths and Weaknesses

Once you've made a list of your life goals, it is important to access your strengths and weaknesses to assess if they are congruent to your overall objectives. Go area wise when you make a list of your strengths and limitations. For instance, devote one page to your professional life, another to your personal life, yet another to your social or spiritual life and so on.

Think carefully and jot down everything you believe you are really good at in the strengths column. List down work skills for which you almost always receive appreciation or think you excel at. Then, list down all the areas that need improvement in your work and life. For instance, you may be a fabulous researcher but lag behind when it comes to time management.

Focus closely on how these strengths and weaknesses tie in with your present life, and if they benefit your larger goals. For instance, one of your social weaknesses can be excessive consumption of alcohol, which may not just affect your social relationships but also punctuality and cognitive skills at work.

Is this adding overall value to your goal fulfillment or is it taking away from it? You'll realize what you need to remove from your life when you make a comprehensive list of your strengths and weaknesses, and that is the first step towards working on it.

Keep in mind that nobody but you is judging you by your responses, so be as honest as you can when it comes to identifying your weaknesses. Keep jotting them down as they come to you.

Observe Your Emotions Closely

Our emotions can be reliable indicators of our strengths and weaknesses. We have the power to reveal what you are good at and not so good at by tapping into our innermost feelings. Learn to closely tune in to your intuition and internal feelings. How do you feel when you perform certain tasks? Do you feel good, happy and relaxed? Or are you more tensed, bored and stressed?

When we do something we like, the feel-good hormones in our body automatically help us feel positive and relaxed. On the other hand, when we dislike doing something, our emotions become more tensed.

For instance, you may be a fabulous researcher when it comes to digging out information from various sources. However, this feel-good sentiment instantly changes into boredom or stress when you have to draft a report based on your research. This means you may be an excellent researcher but writing may not be one of your plus points. When you are able to recognize this by observing a simple shift in emotions, you equip yourself to overcome your limitations.

However, this isn't a thumb rule. Sometimes based on the situation or circumstances we can still be stressed or irritated while doing things we normally enjoy doing and vice-versa.

Analyze Yourself With Respect to Others

While we're always taught that comparing ourselves with others is social blasphemy, it helps us understand and overcome our weaknesses. Willpower can be exercised only when we identify our shortcomings and make a conscious decision to work on it. Sometimes, comparing ourselves with others is unavoidable.

It is alright to view your pluses and shortcomings vis-à-vis others to determine your core strengths and areas of improvement. This isn't judging or getting into a game of one-upmanship. It isn't viewing others as superior or inferior; it is simply an objective analysis of your skills, personality, and habits.

You know where exactly you are placed in comparison to others. Do others write a report as well as you? Are they as deadline oriented as you? Do they score as high on accuracy as you do? These observations and comparisons will help you determine your own strengths and limitations.

Other factors being the same, if others are struggling to complete a report which you have been able to turn in on time, you may be an ace multitasker or possess better time management skills. On the other hand, if everyone has been able to turn in the report on time and you're the one having a tough time completing it, you may be lacking time management skills. This method works for both – identifying strengths and weaknesses.

Focus on Growth Not Perfection

When you study the life patterns of top performers in any field, you'll realize that they don't try to be perfect or good at everything. They are simply focusing on optimizing their potential in their area of interest. Learn to accept the fact that you can't be great at doing everything every time.

Don't pretend to know everything or be good at everything. If a specific weakness is not integral to your life goals, don't stress about it too much. Learn to distinguish the weaknesses are central to your goal from the ones that you can live with. Progress, and not perfection, should be your goal. Improve constantly by challenging yourself rather than wanting to be good at everything.

Evaluate your weekly, monthly and annual performance. You'll know exactly where you are headed with your weaknesses. If working on your weaknesses can impact your performance at work or improve your relationships/life in general, work on it.

Don't be hard on yourself and push yourself to be good at everything. Limitations will be there and you can't expect to overcome all your weaknesses in a short span of time. It is alright to ask for help when you feel the need to work on your weaknesses.

You may have a steel resolve, yet there can be somebody who can help you achieve stellar results by focusing on your strengths and overcoming your weaknesses. You don't become small by reaching out to be people and admitting to your imperfection. If anything, you are taking the first step towards perfection.

It is normal to not be good at everything and ask for help. Don't focus on succeeding alone. Enlist the help of people of caliber who are highly determined themselves. If nothing, their grit will rub off you too.

Focus on Small Victories

Focusing on identifying and overcoming your weaknesses through sheer willpower is not about achieving overnight success. You can't go from being a socially awkward person to a social communications superstar in a day. Be practical. Once you identify your weaknesses and consciously work towards overcoming them, celebrate the small victories instead of being obsessed with the end result.

Your goal may be to knock off 40 pounds from your weight, and that's certainly not a quick process. You will have to remain steadfast and focus on small milestones. How about five pounds a month to begin with? Then when you achieve these small results, set higher goals, say 10 pounds a month.

Go gradually. Celebrate small victories. Applauding yourself for small results will help you aim higher.

How do you master a new language? Do you start speaking fluently after the first session or class? Or do you take baby steps by learning sounds, syllables, basic words and phrases and then full-fledged sentences? This is pretty much how it is about mastering any skill or overcoming a limitation. You won't fly overnight, though you can encourage yourself by celebrating small wins. Each tiny step is a progress in the right direction.

Chapter 2: 7 Powerful Tips To Motivate Yourself

Motivation is a mixture of a whole lot of things that drive you mostly based on an overwhelming desire or intense fear. It is a battle that is being fought in your head, where you believe you can achieve something yet sometimes wonder if you really can. There are several psychological theories and models about what drives us to do things and how we react to incentives and accomplishments. However, in general, motivation is a sense of excitement we feel towards fulfilling a goal.

Here are some tried and tested super tips for keeping your motivation batteries charged all the time.

1. Stay Focused

Focus breeds motivation. When you focus and achieve results, it keeps you motivated for going even further. Distraction, on the other hand, is a serious motivation killer.

There is an interesting anecdote about motivation. Warren Buffet, Bill Gate's dad, and Bill Gates were at a dinner gathering. A guest casually inquired what the trio thought was the most important attribute for success in modern times, and three promptly replied "focus" at precisely the same time. Later, they laughed together because this wasn't an answer the trio had prepared.

We are perpetually flooded with texts, social media feed, and emails, which makes it a challenge to focus on the task at hand without interruptions/distractions. The sheer volume of information we carry in our handheld devices makes focus a daunting prospect.

The best way to focus is by turning off distracting apps, smartphones, and social media notifications, and just work.

2. Look After Yourself Physically

Well yes, motivation and willpower can be mental attributes. However, you also need the physical strength and stamina required for sustaining through the task. This can happen only when you have sufficient reserves of physical energy to tap into.

Do you get tired quickly? Are you getting enough sleep? Are you leading a fit and active life to stay more energized and less lethargic? Do you find yourself becoming sad or lethargic, for no apparent reason?

Get seven to eight hours of sleep every day. Make sure you are consuming balanced and nutritious meals. Avoid sugar, high-calorie meals, processed meals and artificially sweetened products. Opt for raw fruits and vegetables that give you more energy. Chuck depending on nicotine, alcohol or caffeine.

Engage in 30-60 minutes of physical activity such as cycling, running, brisk walking, dancing or playing tennis. Learn to tune in to your body and listen to its needs. It is tough to stay motivated when you are not physically fit to complete tasks. You must feel good about your body and yourself to stay upbeat.

3. Share Your Goals Publically

One of the best ways to stay motivated is to take away all other options by being accountable to others. How about sharing your goals in public or on the social media? You will have no other way but to fulfill your goal to avoid becoming a laughing stock in your social circle.

People are increasing sharing their goals on the social media to give it more accountability. You are making yourself accountable for fulfilling the goal, which is likelier to push you towards achieving it. Imagine stating proudly on the social media that you want to become a few pounds lighter and then going to a family get together a few pounds heavier. Unthinkable, right?

4. Move It From Your Head to a Paper

So you know everything you want to do. It's all there right up in your head, only to be bundled into a chaotic knot. You've got to prepare a presentation, plan your vacation, start your fitness training and much more. However, you don't know how to begin and how to achieve these myriad goals. Kill the uncertainty by putting everything down on paper.

Detailed lists can be organized and efficient while helping you save time by chalking out a clear course of action. You know the exact tasks to be completed, and the action to be taken to finish them. Break down large goals into bite-sized doable chunks.

Make an attractive planner/calendar to schedule specific tasks for the day/week/month. The more detailed and specific you are with putting it down on paper, the easier it becomes for you to organize, follow-up and move on to the next task.

Track your progress. If you've mentioned giving up junk food, put a tick mark against each day you've managed to go without unhealthy treats. Write a motivating note to yourself to keep going.

If you're the more creative sort, use color pencils, stickers, comic strips, motivational quotes or anything uniquely you to mark specific activities. Your planner should inspire you to act. Writing your plans and goals also eliminates the tendency to get distracted and deviated from your goals.

5. Surround Yourself With Action Oriented Folks

The Longevity Project by Howard Friedman analyzed 1000 subjects from their youth until death and arrived at the conclusion that, "the groups you associate with often determine the type of person you become. For people who want improved health, association with other healthy people is usually the strongest and most direct path of change."

Another study revealed that our persona is a reflection of the five people we spend maximum time with. When you fill your life with people whose goals are pretty much aligned with yours, it is less stressful and more fulfilling to manifest these goals.

There is greater positive energy, higher potential for positive change, and more goal sustainability. You can be assured people will be ready to pull you up when you slack and motivate you with their inspiring actions.

Pro tip – find a task buddy whose goals are similar to yours and who can motivate you when you get lazy. It isn't easy to quit when you have a gym buddy or 'quit smoking' buddy playing a tough task master to help you fulfill your goals.

6. Start Your Day On A Positive Note

Starting your day on a positive note is one of the best tricks to keep yourself upbeat and motivated throughout the day. Fill your morning playlist with songs that inspire you. Drink a cup of hot chocolate. Read a few pages of a highly moving biography. Take a hot shower. Start on a wonderful note to pave the way for doing amazing things through the day.

One of the best tips from people who manage to squeeze in a lot in their day is to begin the day early. Get the toughest and lengthiest tasks completed in the morning. Do as much as you can early in the day. Once you're through with the more challenging assignments, everything else will be a breeze. You will be more driven and motivated to finish the task.

Also, prepare for the day's tasks by the previous evening or night, so you don't waste time figuring out what and how it is to be done. Make a list of tasks to be completed the next day.

Have all your documents and files ready. Keep your clothes for the day in place. When you gear up in advance, there's little scope for rush and stress. You feel less chaotic, more organized and much more productive. Being late makes you feel rushed, and can be a huge motivation killer.

7. Make a Happy List

Use any notes/visual application on a smartphone or tablet to make your every own happy list. Keep a list on a loop of everything that makes you smile. You can also write about moments that brought you immense joy during the day at the end of each day. This can keep you excited and determined about your goal.

Track what makes you really upbeat. Keep adding to the list. It can be a cake you baked, a joke you read somewhere, a song you love, a person you really admire or a trip you recently took. The idea is to stoke your spirit and keep you inspired.

Chapter 3: Recognize and Build Your Resilience

While there are plenty of books that endlessly address the concept of persistence, determination, resilience and grit, few bother to tell you how to actually develop these qualities. How does one build the resistance muscle? What is it the separates winners from losers? How do you develop a doer's attitude? How do you survive in the most challenging situations? Here are some proven methods for building resilience and achieving success.

Look At Challenges As Self-Discovery Opportunities

Resilience is about staying upbeat and overcoming the most challenging situations. People tend to discover a lot within themselves during trying times. When you experience hardships and life's tragedies, you develop greater strength, more fulfilling relationships, healthy spirituality, higher gratitude and a greater appreciation for life's gifts.

Imagine what losing their job can do for the wannabe entrepreneur or the travel photography enthusiast? There's so much to explore within ourselves. Adverse situations or so-called tragedies can be blessings in disguise at times. They take us on a route for self-discovery and are capable of bringing out the best, which we didn't even know existed. Treat every adversity as an opportunity and watch your stellar fate unfold!

Open the Heart

Well no, I am not advocating a career as a cardiologist. All I am suggesting is being of service to those in need, which is a brilliant way to stoke your own resilience. You not only feel great about being able to add value to others' lives but also learn to appreciate the gifts you've been blessed with. When you realize you are more fortunate than several people inhabiting the planet, your resilience increases multi-fold.

Research has pointed to the fact that when we engage in acts of kindness, our serotonin (the neurotransmitter used connected with feelings of elation and well-being) becomes more efficient. Thus people who constantly practice acts of kindness are able to use their serotonin much more effectively, which helps them draw from it when they need resilience. When you go out there and find a way to make people smile, you are creating an encouragement bank for yourself too.

Get Comfortable With Discomfort

You are either a green, growing fruit or a ripe, decaying one. Get out of your comfort zone and learn to embrace discomfort if you want to become more resilient. Proactively volunteer to do that presentation if you're a hesitant public speaker, go out there and date if you feel awkward while approaching people from the opposite gender. Push your boundaries, remove the safety net and wake up from the complacency. It is rightly said that "complacency is the foe of courage." It won't be easy but it might be worth it when you realize that things you were afraid of initially aren't such a big deal after all. You can imagine the wonders this can do to your confidence. Make it a daily or weekly habit to do something you usually wouldn't do, and witness how it boosts your resilience power.

Resilient people are never stagnant. They are perpetually challenging themselves and using their varied experiences as sound learning opportunities. These folks realize that true growth is going beyond your comfort zone, and growing. Are you prepared to use your discomfort as a growth catalyst?

Be A Problem Solver

People scoring high on the resilience quotient aren't stuck in the negative thinking mold. They aren't prone to thinking in extremes or paralyzed by excessive self-defeating thoughts. They are also looking for options and solutions to handle the situation more efficiently.

For instance, your supervisor may cut your work hours. While some may see this as an adverse situation where your wages reduce, resilient folks may perceive this as a brilliant opportunity to explore other vocations and job openings. They may sign up for a class to upgrade their skills or register for a part-time/online course or even join a hobby club. In the long haul, this could translate into a favorable career growth that you weren't perceptive enough to imagine when you're work hours were cut back.

Research has pointed to the fact that people who think up solutions for problems instead of brooding over them are better equipped to cope with them. Whenever you come across a new problem, get into the habit of making a quick solutions list of some potential solutions for the newly faced challenge.

Experiment with multiple strategies and concentrate on creating a rational manner for working through regular challenges. Practicing problem-solving skills consistently prepares you to cope with huge challenges ahead. Think out of the box for solutions. Think of different ways to resolve issues rather than magnifying them with your negative thoughts.

Build Support Systems and Connections

Focus on building powerful support systems within your family, friends and social groups. Accept, help, guidance, and support from those who truly care about you and listen to you in a non-judgmental manner. For some people, being a part of faith-based organizations, charity groups, and local support groups works wonders. You can help or assist those in need to strengthen your own resilience.

Being surrounded by caring, encouraging and supportive people often gives you a protective factor during crisis situations. It is important to forge meaningful connections and to be with people you can pour your heart out to. Simply talking to a friend or confidant about the challenges you face may not eliminate them. However, it allows you to open up about your feelings, find support, get encouraging feedback, and come up with solutions to various problems. This in itself can be extremely therapeutic.

Lack of support may lead to developing lesser resilience to life's challenges. Find an inspiring mentor who can help you tide through life's toughest waters. When you're alone, you tend to feel hopeless and discouraged. However, when you have an older/wiser person guiding you, you'll feel more armed to combat life's challenges.

The mentor can be any inspiring, wise and balanced person who can help put things in perspective for you. It can be an older friend, a grandparent, parent, supervisor at work, counselor, coach, or just about anyone whose words have a positive impact of your goal fulfillment.

Find A Strong Purpose

After Candace Lightner's 13-years-old daughter died in a drunk driving encounter, she founded Mothers Against Drunk Driving, or *MADD* as it's popularly known. She converted a tragedy into a life mission or sense of purpose. Disappointed with the light sentence the driver got way with, Lighter dedicated her life to creating a sense of awareness about the hazards of drunk driving.

She resolved firmly on the day of her daughter's death that she would use her loss as a means to fight for needless drunk driving homicides, and bring about a positive change in society. We can often find a sense of purpose in the most trying times and mend a broken system, which ultimately helps us recover. It can be anything from being involved within the community or nurturing your spirituality or being a part of meaningful activities.

Having clear goals and objectives boosts your resilience. Lack of goals decreases resilience and leave you more vulnerable to manipulation, poor choices, and little control over your life, which in turn can lead to anxiety, stress, and depression.

Consider the most important goals in your life. What gives you the strongest sense of purpose in life? What keeps you focused and fulfilled? Make a list of things that you really want to achieve in life. Also, what are the things that detract you from your goals? Try and live your life based on these values, beliefs convictions, and you'll fight lesser battles within yourself.

Cultivate a Sense of Humor

Hard times are all about being able to look at the situation in a lighter vein and laugh. Humor can help you cope with the toughest challenges. Learn to gain a lighter perspective on hard issues. It increases your well-being, physical health and brain dopamine levels, which ultimately boosts the overall health.

During particularly stressful situations, watch s funny film that never fails to make you laugh. Read a laugh-a-minute book or spend time with genuinely humorous people. These techniques can help balance your woes by offering you the much needed comic relief. It is tough to hit the bottom of a despair-filled pit when you're in lighter spirits.

Learn to let go of all inhibitions and laugh at yourself. The supreme ability to avoid taking yourself seriously equips you to face challenges of all kinds with a dazzling smile on your face.

Practice Yoga and Meditation

Meditation is an excellent way to focus, clear the mind and balance thoughts. It helps you tap into your inner spiritual reserves to bring about a harmony between the body, mind, and spirit. When you feel calm, positive and balanced internally, it is easier to draw willpower from within. Meditation also relaxes you, gives you glowing physical health and eliminates stress/nervousness/anxiety.

You don't need to follow an elaborate meditation routine. Even 10-15 minutes of deep breathing or mindful focus will help clear the cobwebs in your mind and award you more peace. Slow down and meditate when you feel too overwhelmed by life's challenges. It won't just bring you to be more calm, but also help you feel in greater control of the situation. A regular meditation practice will allow you to view things in a more objective perspective.

Find a comfortable seating position. Shut your eyes. Focus on taking deep breaths. Work on a single body part at a time. Do away with all the noise and distractions around you. If possible, fill the room with positive, uplifting paraphernalia like scented candles, incense sticks, and fresh flowers. Take deep breaths and observe the feeling on each part of the body by focusing completely on it. Meditation helps you develop a more detached outlook to the problems in your life, which helps in coming up with solutions more effectively.

A Harvard Medical School study revealed that people who engage in a regular practice of yoga compared to other fitness techniques were less likely to outbursts and more efficient in tackling challenges. There is also greater physical and mental endurance/ strength in hold body postures. Your body is begging you to stop while you are still sustaining the posture. It grows your ability to simply stick with uncomfortable situations and find ways to stay peaceful, unaffected and resilient.

Be Action Oriented

Being idle breeds lower resilience, but being proactive and action-oriented in handling your challenges head-on enhances your capability to deal with the toughest situations. Avoid ruminating over self-defeating thoughts or notions. Instead, get up and take action to resolve the situation.

For instance, you have written a wonderful novel that no one has really shown an interest in publishing. Your worth doesn't depend on the opinion others have about your novel. Relying on publishers to accept or like you book may not be the best option. Take pride in your work. Keep trying to find a publisher.

However, if you're the more action-oriented sort, you simply self-publish the book instead of trying hard to see it published by a big ticket publisher. Do something new and path-breaking if the old methods don't seem to work.

If you are fired from work (so are hundreds of others, you aren't alone), pull up your socks and look for another job. Find something that offers you a greater sense of value, happiness, and fulfillment, even it means chalking an altogether differ career path. Though it may not be obvious initially, losing a job you hate can be one of the best blessings in disguise. Focus on the positives, keep things in perspective and head towards a resolution.

Chapter 4: Being Accountable for Your Actions

Accountability is the aftermath of responsibility. It is a deep-seated willingness to answer for the consequences arising out of one's choices, behavior, decisions, and actions. When you hold yourself accountable, you stop shifting blame from yourself to other people and get out of the excuse-making mindset. Instead, there is a greater tendency to take the hit when your choices lead to unflattering outcomes, which in turn increases your resilience.

Accountability also means responsibility towards fulfilling your goals.

Here are some ways to hold yourself accountable for you actions and goals.

Own Up to the Truth

No one goes by without messing up at times. It is usual for people to mess up. However, you are messing it up even more by attempting to cover it up. Remember the impeachment price Bill Clinton paid for not speaking the truth in front of a grand jury.

Well, be wise and save yourself the stress by admitting to your mistakes. Untruths won't take you a long way. No one, including you, believes fabricated stories anyway. The lack of conviction is pretty evident. You might as well earn respect by admitting to your mess up front and try to rectify the situation instead of having people talk behind your back and make it worse. Owning up to your acts and accepting responsibility for the consequences builds your resilience muscle big time.

Develop a Self Growth Plan

Open yourself up to knowledge, revelations, and reviews for a strong self-development plan that increases your resilience. Use the knowledge you gain through various sources and apply it to your life and professional growth.

Set aside a fixed budget and number of hours for self-development through which you can hold yourself accountable for your actions and progress. You can utilize these funds for purchasing books, listening to audio podcasts, attending industry related seminars and being a part of events, which are in sync with your goals.

Continue to reflect on your commitments, goals, and performances. We must make an effort to document our personal commitments for tracking results – both for professional and personal goals. When you track exactly how much you eat, spend, and work out – you become increasingly conscious about your actions and directly accountable for them. Use this premise for tracking your progress.

Set Micro Objectives

Micro goals allow you to work on easily chewable digest goals at a time, which can be expanded later. They serve as building blocks for several bigger goals. For instance, your goal is clear your massive credit card debt. You start with a micro goal of making slightly bigger than minimum payments on the balance. Gradually, you start increasing the payment to reach your bigger goal of being debt-free. Every month, you have payments that are higher than the previous month (which is a micro goal) until eventually you reach the ultimate goal (being debt-free).Long term goals are easier to achieve when you have tangible short-term strategies.

Everything that makes its way into your task list should not be mistaken for a micro goal. Cleaning your desk or responding to a client may not be a micro goal unless it contributes to a larger goal. Micro goals increase your willpower while you inch your way towards larger goals.

Set Clear Goals

One of the biggest blunders most entrepreneurs and other people make is shying away from setting clear goals. Everyone wants to grow and overcoming challenges. However clearly defining your goals makes you better equipped to deal with life's challenges. If you don't know what you want, how will you know the course to be charted and the obstacles to be overcome to get there?

If you don't know where exactly you want to go, how will you use the roadmap to take you there? How will you know how to prepare yourself for the tough situations ahead? How will you be able to withstand the setbacks and increase your willpower during the goal-fulfillment process? If you haven't defined exactly what you are looking for, you have little right to be disappointed when you don't get it.

Be laser-specific while setting goals. By how much to you want your sales to increase? What revenue figure are you looking to clock at the end of the year? How many pounds do you want to shed at the end of this month? How do plan to lose 10 pounds in the next 45 days? The more elaborate and detailed your goals, the higher are your chances at succeeding in achieving them.

Be Specific

Make yourself accountable before you demand accountability from others. One of the best ways to achieve this is to be being extremely specific and clear in your communication. Ambiguity is the nemesis of accountability. When setting the agenda or planning goals, keep it very specific. For instance, instead of stating that the proposal will be mailed to the team by the month end, agree to mail it by 6 p.m. PST by Friday,

March 31st, 2017 in its final version. This way you are agreeing to very specific deadlines, for which you can be held accountable.

Chapter 5: Learn Patience and Tolerance

We're trained to believe from a very young age that patience is a huge virtue. However, the number of people who actually practice patience and tolerance is staggeringly low. The good news is – patience isn't something that we're born with or without. It can be cultivated over consistent practice and conscious effort. We can condition ourselves to be more patient and tolerant.

Patience and tolerance are pretty much like several other hard acquired virtues. The more you invest in practicing tolerance, the higher your patience/tolerance raise. Since patience is a trainable and acquirable skill, here are some amazing tips to help you cultivate patience, and thus increase your resilience power.

See Through Someone Else's Perspective

Though it seems easy to judge someone else or snap at them for something they've done, try and look at things from their perspective. Step back for a bit and look at things more objectively when they seem overwhelming.

Free yourself from personal biases, opinions or disappointments, and focus on resolving the issue. Losing your cool may only make the situation worse. Resilience is all about having the patience to see your vision through, even if it means showing seemingly huge and unreal reserves of patience/tolerance.

Be strong and learn to handle pressure. Be wise and concentrate on solutions rather than aggravating the problem. Keep your eyes firmly fixated on the larger picture, while connecting the dots to arrive at a solution, which will help you build your self-esteem and resilience.

Keep Telling Yourself Things Take Time

Keep reminding yourself that all good things in life take time. Nothing that is worth having comes in an instant, and if it does, it may really not be worth having. Folks who are impatient want everything quick and hence go about achieving their goals in a rush.

Think about some of the happiest moments and biggest achievements in your life. Weren't they instances where your tolerance/patience paid off manifold? Wasn't it the time you worked diligently and consistently to fulfill your goal that really wasn't temporarily gratifying but hugely satisfying in the long run? Think about the long, leisurely hours spent in the company of a parent or grandparent. Would you able to make those wonderful memories if you were impatient?

It takes dedication, patience and time to reach your goals, and things that hold a high relevance in your life. While nice things may not always come to folks who wait, but a majority of good things that do come to you do not come right away.

It requires a high level of maturity to understand/accept the facts that even if it takes time, you will eventually get what you want. Patience is much like a mental skill that once acquired will never let you down. Train yourself to accept what can't be changed before it throws your life off the gear.

Slow Down

While we often have a rush-around tendency in order to get a lot done in a short span of time, it is important to learn to slow down and let things take their time. Stop right in your track and take deep breaths before making the next move or deciding your next course of action.

For instance, the next time you find yourself caught in choc-a-bloc traffic or a serpentine supermarket queue, try not get worked up. Listen to soothing music, enjoy the scenic view outside, people watch or simply fill your mind with positive thoughts. Getting impatient or intolerant will not help the queue move faster, so there's really no use getting worked up. Instead, just enjoy the inevitable inconvenience by replacing it with more meaningful moments.

Take a break and do nothing if it seems too overwhelming. Just sit still and think. Avoid watching television or listening to music or reading. It can be mighty challenging when you're starting out. However, by taking time out and slowing down, it can be easier to connect with your deeper selves and develop a patient and tolerant attitude, which in turn can help you build your resilience muscle.

Stop holding others and yourself to highly unrealistic or unattainable standards. The world would be rosy perfect if dishes didn't break, children didn't drop things or computer systems never crashed or people didn't err at all. However, that isn't the way things work. Don't expect the world to run hitch-free. Give yourself a nice break and go out and breathe in the fresh air.

Cope With the Unexpected

Yes, we make the grandest plans for our life, but things, unfortunately, do not always go as planned. Your patience and tolerance threshold will increase (and so will your resilience) once you learn to accept unexpected twists in your life with grace. Keep your goals realistic, and be prepared to tackle with the unwanted turns.

When you blow up at a child for accidently dropping a drink, you're not in sync with the fact that people are imperfect. Even considering the fact that it is not an isolated occurrence but a recurring one that is caused by callousness and neglect, is your screaming going to resolve the issue? The issue will be better addressed if you show restraint and act logically, with as much scope for discussion as possible. Keeping a balanced mind and controlled attitude increases your resilience. Your threshold for challenges goes even higher.

The 10 Second Technique

This is one expert technique that can be used virtually in any challenge you face in life. The ten-second rule has multiple applications and can be used in any situation where you think you're tempted to run out of patience. This is how it works – each time your patience reserves feel like they're drying up, stop for ten seconds and reflect on the choice you are going to make. Is it a sensible choice? Is it right? Will it help resolve the issue? More often than not, it is likely to help you make a balanced and rational decision.

Try and think about the endless applications this technique has in our everyday life. From buying into unwanted cell phone options to signing up for multiple credit cards to giving in to an overpromising mutual fund, it prevents you from acting mindlessly. Give yourself the gift of the powerful ten seconds reflection.

Grow Plants

Growing plants and watching them flower by nurturing them each day is a brilliant tip for developing patience. When you witness each growth stage of a seed you planted, it instills a deep sense of joy, balance. and patience. You come to appreciate the fact that all good things in life, such as a flowering/thriving plant, take time.

There might be complications or delays or temporary challenges. However, it is an inevitable aspect of your life that is to be dealt with rather than giving up. You realize it is worth it to overcome all the setbacks to experience your patience blossom into a beautiful plant.

Spending time with children is another wonderful way to develop high patience reserves. Try to let go and laugh frequently.

Practice Kindness and Empathy

There are times when we become increasingly impatient with people, especially when they behave in a manner that doesn't fulfill our expectations. There is a lot of stress involved because we are solely focused on our needs, without taking the other person's point of view into consideration.

Demonstrating empathy and compassion for other people is the basis of tolerance. Sometimes all that's needed to diffuse a potentially tensed situation is less focus on our expectations and a little more empathy towards others. Take time to be kind to others and empathize with them.

For instance, your subordinate may have had a really horrible day before getting to work, which is why they may not be performing up to the mark or may appear distracted. They may not have understood your instructions correctly or may be battling an issue you know nothing about. Try and understand things from their perspective by empathizing with them before judging them or terming them incompetent.

Displaying a little more compassion can go a long way in resolving the issue. It immediately nullifies any tension and lets you tackle the problem with greater patience and understanding. Try and understand people before judging them o develop higher tolerance levels.

Chew Your Food

Another ace patience and resilience building tip. People who chew their morsels slowly and mindfully, while overlooking their hunger pangs tend to eat less on the whole. They are known to possess greater patience and savor their meals even more. Impatient eaters, on the other hand, tend to be overweight, owing to failure to delay gratification.

The simple practice of eating slowly can help you tremendously in most life areas such as conditioning you to be more patient and less reactive.

Chapter 6: 6 Smart Tips for Staying Positive During the Toughest Times

1. Find the Positive in Every Situation

Every negative situation comes with some positivity attached to it, even though we may not have the foresight to recognize it at the onset. Ask yourself positive and solution-oriented questions. We are prone to asking ourselves questions such as have I made a mistake? Am I a failure? Or what are the terrible consequences of my mistake? However, instead try and ask yourself questions such as what is the one good thing emerging from this seemingly challenging situation? What is the hidden opportunity in this setback?

This will offer you way more options and a solid plan of action than being stuck with how you suck at everything you do or how your luck has completely run out. The defeatist mentality will do little to improve the situation for you. Stay strong and build your resilience by asking yourself the appropriate questions.

It won't be easy to employ fake optimistic thinking when you are in an emotionally volatile state of mind. Allow yourself to feel a bit shocked and overwhelmed, which is a natural process, before returning to a more balanced state of mind where you ask yourself the right questions. Do not force yourself to think positively. Just give it time after you've gone through the turmoil, and come back with more hopeful options.

2. Avoid Thinking in Extremes

It is easy to put things in a wrong perspective when you are highly stressed or anxious. We all have an inherent tendency to imagine the worst in any situation or to make a mountain of a molehill.

If someone doesn't answer our call or return our message simply because they are busy in a meeting or driving, we assume they don't want to talk to us or worse – something terrible has happened to them. We create these large mountains of fear, terror, and despair in the minds, which often don't exist in reality.

The best way to handle this thinking that often goes out of hand is to say stop aloud to halt your thinking right in its tracks. Once you've put an end to this chain of negative thoughts, take a deep breath from the belly and sit still. Focus on nothing else but the breathing. Calm the mind, body, and spirit.

Try and gain a more balanced perspective about your thoughts by speaking to someone who knows you well. You can get a more grounded view of the situation simply by venting out or gaining a rational input. Things may really not be as terrible as you're imaging them to be, and someone else telling you this may help you actually believe it. Widen your vision to incorporate less extreme thinking. Will the setback matter to you in the next 5 weeks, months or years? This will give you a good idea about how to treat the seemingly challenging situation.

3. Be Grateful

Remember, whatever situation you are in currently, someone somewhere is dealing with far worse challenges than you think. Your life, with all its problems and setbacks, may be a dream life for someone. Think about people who struggle to get two square meals a day or those who live in war-ridden zones and simply await their death or those who battle terminal illnesses and simply wish to live a few days longer.

People go through far worse than what you are complaining about. Though you may be experiencing a tough time, be ever grateful for the gifts you've been blessed with. Be thankful that worse things did not happen. This doesn't, of course, mean that you totally deny that something bad has occurred. It simply means, acknowledge the bad but be grateful it wasn't worse. Find positivity in the situation.

Always remember to express gratitude towards people who have shaped your life. Do not take the simple things you've been blessed with, such a roof over your head, a bed to sleep comfortably or a job that helps you earn a decent living, for granted. However much you hate your boss or job, keep in mind that it pays your rent and prevents you from leading an uncomfortable life on the streets. There are things to be grateful for in the bleakest situations. Recognize these things and build on them to help you tide through the toughest life situations.

4. Things Will Be Sorted

Sometimes in our bid to resolve a challenging situation, we complicate it even further and then lower our resilience in the bargain. Think about how nature tackles challenges. Trees become barren and desolate during winters. However, times changes, seasons change and they are back to their lush, blossoming freshness in spring.

Though it may currently not be the most thriving spring time in your life, this doesn't mean it's never going to be spring for you. The depressing and cold winters will slowly fade and be replaced by flourishing spring blossoms. It's the law of nature – day follows night. Similarly, it can't be darkness in your life forever. Even if you don't realize it now, trust that things will fall into place by themselves eventually. Think how every tough situation happens for a reason, and how the reason for every biting cold and uncomfortable winter is the spring that follows.

Tiding through tough times becomes relatively easier when we are patient enough to realize that what we become why waiting for our goals is way more important that achieving those goals itself. Resilience goes a long way in transforming you as a person. While waiting for spring, you aren't struggling but actually preparing yourself for something way bigger and better than you imagined.

5. Keep Yourself Occupied

Participate in activities that are therapeutic and rejuvenating, while helping you lift your spirits. Activities such as cooking, sketching, blogging, running, cycling and knitting can be highly engaging and effective in keeping your mind off the challenging situation.

Being busy in something you're insanely passionate about or have a deep interest in can help iron out negative thoughts and anxious situations to help you gain a more balanced perspective. Focus on any hobby that brings you joy and see it through its completion. Whether it's knitting, gardening, blogging or painting – create wonderful things and don't give up until you complete it. You will not just witness a marked improvement in your skill levels, but your stress level will also drop down.

Another great way to combat overwhelming situations is to unwind with a bunch of entertainment/recreation options.

How about enjoying a session of binge watching on Netflix with your friends and unlimited popcorn? How about having friends over and making delicious finger foods for them? How about the long forgotten game nights that you did during your more carefree days?

This strategy isn't about escaping your troubles or running away from facing the situation/troubles. It is about avoiding being excessively preoccupied and anxious about a situation to the point of making it even worse for yourself. Give yourself some time off, trust things will be sorted and come back with a more balanced perspective.

6. Start Your Days On a Positive Note

The manner in which you start your day establishes the tone for the entire day. To feel good and positive throughout the day, start on an upbeat note. This is especially true when you are in the midst of a rather challenging situation.

Don't start by thinking about the negative things at full speed and expand the tension or perceived loss. This will throw things off the gear quickly. On the contrary, begin your day by moving along gradually. Have an uplifting or meaningful conversation with yourself. Talk to someone you trust. Spend some time reading inspiring stuff early in the day. Listen to something motivating that stays with you through the day.

Listen to uplifting podcasts while eating your breakfast or commuting to work. Make every moment count in your quest for positivity and notice how your entire day goes wonderfully well, which in turn helps reduce the stress of the challenging situation while boosting your resilience.

Building on the same tip, another great way to cope with tough situations is to be more in the present than future. It becomes considerably simpler to access our positive feelings and stay grounded when we live more mindfully in the present moment rather than constantly worrying about the future.

Worries increase manifold when we let our concerns for the future take over us. It doesn't help to keep replaying past mistakes and fails on a loop. This will only drag you to lower levels of pessimism.

Take one moment at a time if things feel too overwhelming. Instead of worrying yourself to death about finding a new job after being laid off from the previous one, try and plan to get through the day one action at a time. Go through each moment in a balanced and mindful manner.

Create a day wise plan of action. It may be drafting an impressive resume on day one, sending across copies to your LinkedIn and other contacts the next day, preparing yourself for a couple of interviews in the next few days and so on. Things may not happen overnight but the very fact that you're taking concrete action in the right direction will give you a feeling of confidence and hopefulness.

Reconnect with moments rather than losing your equilibrium. Focus on everything that's happening around you with more mindfulness. Use your senses to the fullest to see, hear, smell, taste and touch the wonders around you. Feel the beauty of nature. Feel the power in your feet as they carry you from one place to another. Establish and recognize a sense of reconnection with the moment so you see its positive effects to help you tide through the toughest times.

Chapter 7: Stellar Tips to Help You Practice Effective Time Management

We all have 24 hours in a day and yet, isn't it astounding how some people manage to pack in so much into their day or have enough time to complete all their tasks while others struggle with even half of it? Are you the one always rushing from one task to other, without ever finishing them? What are the ones who manage to pack in much more in a day have that the rushaholics do not? Effective time management skills. Here are some actionable, easy to follow and highly efficient time management tips to help you become a much-envied multi-tasker.

Prioritize Tasks

One of the most effective time management tips is to prioritize your task list. Make a checklist of tasks on the basis of urgent and important. There will be some tasks that are both urgent and important, which will need immediate attention.

Some tasks may only be urgent, which may also need to be tackled immediately, while others may be important but not urgent (so you know you will have to do them eventually though not immediately). The not urgent and not important tasks can be assigned least priority. This saves us from dedicating wasteful time towards low priority tasks that can wait.

Try and get your daily/weekly task list ready a day or week before you actually go about completing it. This helps you set things in order beforehand and avoids wasting time that can be devoted to finishing the task. Nothing kills productivity like regular procrastination bouts. Get your task list in place and start working to enjoy a more balanced personal and professional life.

Create realistic deadlines for tasks at hand and try your best to stick to them. Aim to complete it before the actual deadline so you have a few buffer days to take into account any unforeseen exigencies. Reward yourself periodically for meeting tough deadlines.

Delegate Responsibilities

It is humanly impossible for us to everything every time. Sometimes, we take on more than we can chew and creating complicated situations for ourselves in the bargain. Learn to leverage time, skills and effort by delegating tasks. This way you only reduce your stress and workload but also create an able and dependable workforce for the future.

Delegation doesn't translate into escaping from your responsibilities. It just means you are smart and savvy enough to assign tasks to people on the basis of their skills than face a burnout yourself. Spend some time identifying the strengths and weaknesses of people. Know their primary motivators, fears, aspirations, passions, abilities, and then hand over responsibilities corresponding to these attributes.

Multitasking has become an oft-used and abused term in recent times. While multitasking may seem like an efficient way to get a lot done in a short span of time, it can also be a huge productivity compromiser. Truth be told – we achieve better results when we are able to focus our energies on a single task at a time. Avoid falling into the glamorous sounding multitasking trap and learn to train others for increasing productivity and efficiency.

Learn To Say No

Resilience is also the ability to stand up for yourself and say no when you know you're already occupied with too many things or just do not think the task is worth it. For instance, a co-worker may want you to fill in for him/her during his/he leave, but you already have a pile of your own projects awaiting completion. In such circumstances, you may have to say a firm yet polite no without worrying about what people will think about you.

Say no to tasks that sap your time and energy or deviate/distract you from the more important tasks. You may have an important presentation the next morning and you've spent the entire previous day preparing for it. A friend may want to chill out with you after work but you are tired and need to fresh for the next day's presentation. What should you do? Politely refuse and try and meet up some other time when you're more relaxed and de-stressed.

Saying no to people is a sign of strength and confidence. It doesn't mean you don't respect other or their wishes. It simply means you respect yourself enough to be taken for granted or to be forced to do something that doesn't figure in your current list of priorities.

Don't overpromise or make false promises when you know you can't fulfill them just to keep the other person happy. Be assertive and say no when you mean no. This leaves no scope for misunderstandings or accusations.

Keep Everything Tidy

This may seem like a pedestrian tip but it's astounding how many people actually fail to implement something as basic as tidying up their work desk, cupboard, computer system and other stuff to easy access things that are important. Tidying up boosts not just your physical space but also mental energy. It keeps your mind organized, clutter-free and balanced, thus increasing your resilience in the bargain.

When things around you are in order, it becomes easy to segregate the high priority/important tasks from ones that can wait. Write everything you want to do in a place where you can spot it prominently, say a notice board or fridge. You'll be able to glance it quickly and conveniently and know what tasks lay ahead of you instead of missing them and facing the heat later.

Be Calm and Keep Things in the Right Perspective

Effective time management is all about keeping things in order, even mentally. The most important thing for practicing sound time management skills and resilience is to stay calm and keep stress levels at their minimum. Easier said than done you say? Not really.

Create a few rules for yourself. For instance, you won't work on more than two projects at a time or you will refuse to take on assignments that do not contribute to your overall, larger goal or you will take risks to delegate tasks so you find your leaders and more.

Being overwhelmed by multiple tasks is extremely daunting. The world doesn't crash if you take it easy sometimes or fail to complete a task, especially if you haven't failed to prioritize the task to the best of your efforts. Sometimes, things do not really go as planned and that's alright.

Take some time to pause and get a hold of your life if the rush to finish everything seems too overwhelming. It is fine to call it quits for the day, and start afresh the next day even at the cost of missing a few deadlines if you don't make it a pattern. Clarify your perspective on your life, goals, and priorities, and keep your actions in sync with this clear vision.

Conclusion

Thank you for downloading the book *Willpower How To Discover The Hidden Strength Within Yourself.*

I sincerely hope this book was able to help you develop greater resilience, build your willpower muscle, and fulfill all your goals by tiding through the most challenging and fortitude-testing situations.

The next step is to simply follow all the actionable steps, wisdom nuggets, practical pointers and expert tips mentioned in the book. You have access to the best tips in the world for improving your life and fulfilling your goals. However, reading without application is pointless. Go out there and do everything mentioned in the book and witness your life change gradually but definitively.

Lastly, if you really enjoyed reading this book, please take the time to share your thoughts and post a review on Amazon. It will be highly appreciated.

Here's to the superpower that's present in all us – Willpower!